W9-AJP-832

Red

Flying Foxes

and Other Bats

Book Author: Sheri Reda

For World Book:

Editorial: Paul A. Kobasa, Maureen Liebenson, Scott Richardson, Christine Sullivan

Research: Andy Roberts, Loranne Shields

Graphics and Design: Melanie Bender, Sandra Dyrlund

Photos: Tom Evans, Sylvia Ohlrich

Permissions: Janet Peterson

Indexing: David Pofelski

Proofreading: Anne Dillon

Pre-press and Manufacturing: Carma Fazio, Anne Fritzinger, Steve Hueppchen, Madelyn Underwood

For information about other World Book publications, visit our Web site at http://www.worldbook.com, or call 1-800-WORLDBK (967-5325).

For information about sales to schools and libraries, call 1-800-975-3250 (United States); 1-800-837-5365 (Canada).

World Book, Inc.
233 N. Michigan Avenue
Chicago, IL 60601
U.S.A.

Library of Congress Cataloging-in-Publication Data

Flying foxes and other bats.
    p. cm. -- (World Book's animals of the world)
    Includes bibliographical references (p.   ).
    ISBN 0-7166-1262-3 -- ISBN 0-7166-1261-5
      1. Bats--Juvenile literature. 2. Flying foxes--Juvenile literature.
    I. World Book, Inc. II. Series.

    QL737 .C5F59 2005
    599.4--dc22

                                        2004011340

Printed in Malaysia
1 2 3 4 5 6 7 8 09 08 07 06 05

Picture Acknowledgments: Cover: © Theo Allofs, Corbis; © Stephen Dalton, Photo Researchers; © David Lazenby, Animals Animals; © Kim Taylor, Bruce Coleman Inc.

© Theo Allofs, Corbis 5, 25; © Stephen Dalton, Photo Researchers 15; © Roger De La Harpe, Animals Animals 31; © Michael Durham 33; © Bruce Farnsworth, PlaceStockPhoto.com 53; © Michael & Patricia Fogden, Corbis 51; Michael & Patricia Fogden, Minden Pictures 37; © Eric & David Hosking, Corbis 4, 13; © Mark & Selena Kiser, Bat Conservation International 59; © Stephen J. Krasemann, Bruce Coleman Collection 35; © Wayne Lawler, Photo Researchers 45; © David Lazenby, Animals Animals 2, 27; © Joe McDonald, Tom Stack & Associates 17; © Mark Moffett, Minden Pictures 57; © Juan Manuel Renjifo, Animals Animals 47; © James P. Rowan 29, 55; © Dan Suzio, Photo Researchers 39; © Kim Taylor, Bruce Coleman Collection/Natural Selection 19; © Kim Taylor, Bruce Coleman Inc. 5, 23; © B.G. Thomson, Photo Researchers 7, 61; © Merlin Tuttle, Photo Researchers 41, 43, 49; © Peter Weimann, Animals Animals; 21.

Illustrations: WORLD BOOK illustrations by John Fleck 11, 18.

World Book's Animals of the World

Flying Foxes
and Other Bats

I can't find my glasses! Oh, I'm wearing them.

World Book, Inc.
a Scott Fetzer company
Chicago

Contents

I'm a megabat!

Don't you wish you could hang out with me?

Do you think I'm cute? The flowers LOVE me!

What Is a Bat?

Bats are mammals that can fly like birds. Birds, however, hatch from eggs that their mother lays. But bats, like other mammals, are born able to breathe air and digest food on their own. A bat does not need a lengthy period inside an egg to develop these abilities.

Once a bat is born, its mother nurses it with milk that she makes. She feeds the young bat until it is able to hunt or gather its own food.

Like many mammals, bats have furry bodies. Unlike other mammals, however, bats have wings. Their wings are not feathered, like those of birds. Instead, a bat's wings are made of skin stretched over its bones.

Most bats are nocturnal, or active at night. During the day, nocturnal bats hang upside down by their claws in a sheltered spot and rest or sleep.

Flying foxes are a kind of bat. Their long, furry snouts make them look like foxes, but they are not closely related to foxes at all.

Indian flying fox
roosting

Where in the World Do Flying Foxes and Other Bats Live?

Bats live in many different types of habitats, or places. In fact, the only areas in which bats do not live are Antarctica and the Arctic.

Flying foxes are large bats that live in the tropical regions of Africa, Australia, and Asia. They do not migrate but, instead, stay in this habitat year round. They also stay active year round. They fly from place to place, looking for roosts and food. They feed on the pollen and nectar of the buds and blossoms of fruit trees. They also feed on the juice of fruits.

When flying foxes need a place to rest, they roost together in the branches of large trees.

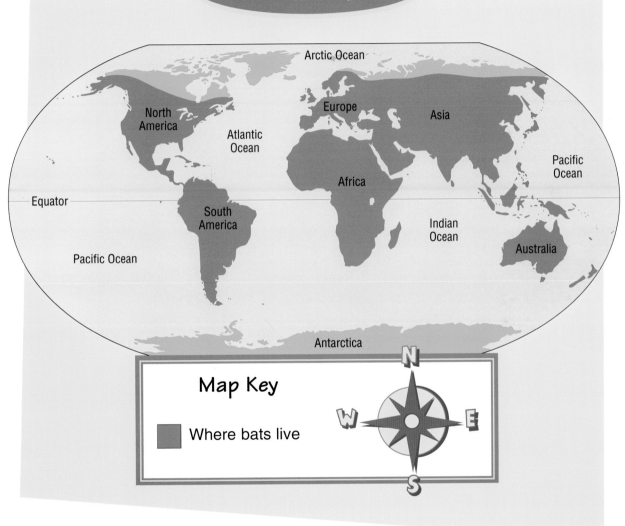

World Map

Arctic Ocean

North America

Atlantic Ocean

Europe

Asia

Pacific Ocean

Africa

Equator

South America

Indian Ocean

Pacific Ocean

Australia

Antarctica

Map Key

Where bats live

N
W
E
S

9

Are Bat Skeletons Like the Skeletons of Other Mammals?

Yes, the skeletons of bats do resemble the skeletons of other mammals. A bat has hands, as do many other mammals. But, a bat's hands are not "just like" other hands—they act as wings. Each hand on a bat has a thumb and four very long fingers. The bones of the fingers support the flexible skin of the wings.

Some types of bats have tails, as do some mammals. And, like most other mammals, bats have legs. But bats' legs are usually weak. A few kinds of bats may use their legs and arms to walk, but many kinds do not walk at all. Instead, they use their legs only to hang from their roost. A bat's foot has five toes, each with a rounded, pointed claw that allows the animal to hang from a crevice or twig.

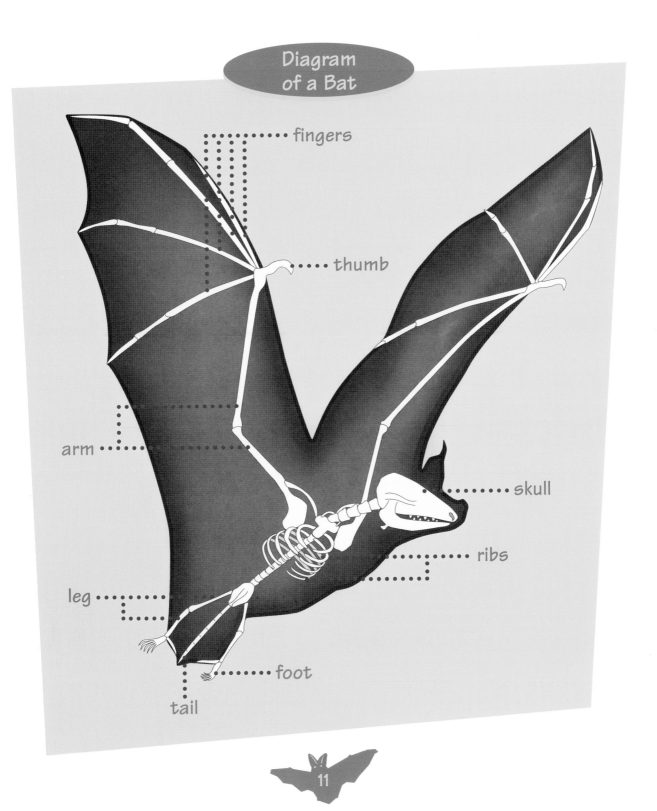

Diagram
of a Bat

fingers

thumb

arm

skull

ribs

leg

foot

tail

11

Are Bats Big or Little?

There are more than 900 species (kinds) of bats. Some are very big. Others are tiny. Kitti's hog-nosed bat, for example, is only a little larger than a bumblebee. The combined length of this bat's head and body is around 1 inch (2.5 centimeters), while a bumblebee might be around ¾ inch (1.9 centimeters) long. The Kitti's hog-nosed bat is not only the smallest kind of bat—it is one of the smallest mammals in the world. On the other hand, the largest bat in North America, the hoary bat, has a wingspan of 16 inches (40.6 centimeters).

Both of those bats are small compared to flying foxes. Flying foxes are the largest kinds of bats. The wingspan of a flying fox can stretch up to 6 feet (1.8 meters). A spectacled flying fox, like the one in the picture, can have a wingspan of nearly 5 feet (1.5 meters). No wonder flying foxes and other fruit bats belong to a group known as Megachiroptera, or the "megabats."

Spectacled flying fox

13

Do Flying Foxes Really Fly?

Yes! Flying foxes and other bats are the only mammals that can fly. Their wings are actually extra-long arms and fingers covered with skin that stretches to the sides of their bodies and legs. In fact, scientists classify all bats into the order Chiroptera, which comes from Greek words meaning "hand" and "wing."

Bats that fly slowly have short, wide wings that help them make sharp turns. Bats that fly quickly have long, narrow wings.

To fly, bats stretch out their arms and fingers and pull the skin of their wings tight. They flap their wings to move through the air. They move their arms and fingers to adjust the shape of their wings to make dips, dives, and turns.

Indian flying fox
in flight

What Kinds of Sounds Do Flying Foxes Make?

Flying foxes make many types of sounds. They are often very noisy—squawking and chattering while they roost.

Other bats make noises, too. They make warning calls and greeting calls to other bats. Some calls sound like honks or chirps, while others sound like hisses.

Most bats also make very high-pitched noises. These noises are so high in pitch (the highness or lowness of a sound) that humans are unable to hear them. In the 1930's, scientists were able to detect these bat noises for the first time by using special recording instruments.

Little brown bats

How Do Flying Foxes and Other Bats See?

Flying foxes have large eyes, and they can see better than most other bats. They are more active during the day than are most bats. Flying foxes use their eyesight to help them move about their habitat.

Most other bats, such as the long-eared bat shown to the right, fly at night and need another way to "see" their surroundings. Instead of relying upon their eyesight, they use sounds to help them figure out where they are and where they are going. They send out their high-pitched sounds and listen to the way the sounds bounce back to them. The echoes tell the bats how near they are to other objects. This is called echolocation *(EHK oh loh KAY shuhn)*.

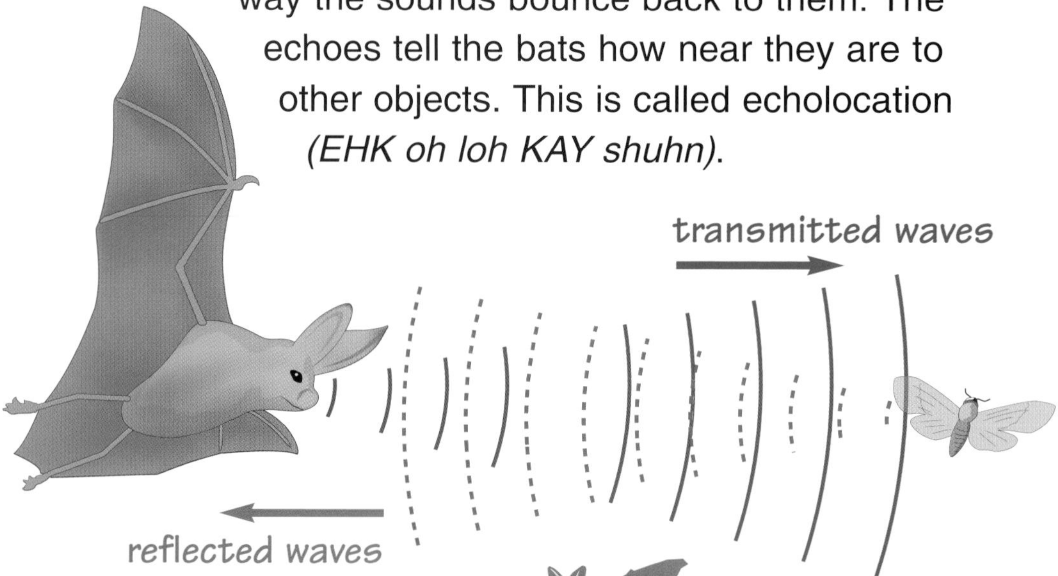

transmitted waves

reflected waves

18

A long-eared bat
hunting a moth

What Do Flying Foxes Eat?

Flying foxes belong to the family known as fruit bats. They sometimes eat nectar and pollen but, usually, flying foxes eat juice that they squeeze out of fruit. When a flying fox smells ripe fruit, it swoops down and bites into it. It then chews the fruit to a pulp and presses the pulp up against the roof of its mouth, squeezing out the juice. It swallows the juice, but spits out the fruit's pulp, skin, and seeds.

Flying foxes eat mainly such fruits as wild figs, which are not grown in orchards. But they also eat such fruits as mangoes, bananas, and papayas, and they will sometimes do a great deal of damage to orchards in which these fruits are being grown. As a result, flying foxes are considered by farmers to be pests. Compared with fruit diseases and insect pests, however, flying foxes cause very little damage to orchards.

Aldabra flying fox
eating fruit

How Do Flying Foxes Help Plants?

Flying foxes have special relationships with many kinds of plants. They help spread the seeds of these plants, allowing them to grow in new areas. Flying foxes often carry the fruit they find to another place to eat. While eating this fruit, they may drop seeds on the ground. Further, the seeds they do swallow are not digested and are eliminated with their waste. The seeds end up on the ground and some of them grow into new plants.

Flying foxes also help to pollinate plants. Some flying foxes eat nectar from flowers. They then carry the pollen that gets stuck to their face from one flower to another flower. This pollinates the flowers—a process that must occur if the flower is to produce fruits and seeds.

Fruit bats with flowers

Where Do Flying Foxes Hang Out?

Like many other kinds of bats, flying foxes live together in groups called colonies. They often travel together from their roost to feeding areas. When they have eaten all the fruit in one place, they fly to other areas where there is more ripe fruit.

When flying foxes are resting, they hang upside down from the high branches of trees. Often, hundreds of bats hang next to each other on a single tree. When it is cold and raining, they fold their wings around their bodies like shawls. When it gets hot, their wings can be used like fans.

Sometimes, so many bats huddle together that they have to fight for space. Over time, the movements made as they struggle strip most of the leaves from their roosting tree.

Group of flying foxes

Do Flying Foxes Ever Turn Right-side Up?

Flying foxes and other bats spend a lot of their time upside down. But, they turn themselves right-side up, as well. For instance, many types of female bats are right-side up when they give birth, and bats almost always turn right-side up to get rid of waste.

Of course, when a bat flies it is right-side up and facing forward. And most bats land at their roost right-side up as well. Flying foxes are clumsy when they land, however. They look as if they are crashing into their perch. Other bats can land smoothly on their feet. They land right-side up and swing themselves upside down. Some bats are so acrobatic that they can flip themselves upside down in the air before they land on their perch.

Spectacled flying fox

How Do Flying Foxes Care for Their Young?

Flying foxes and most other bats have one baby at a time. When it is time to give birth, the mother bats often leave their roost to go to a nursery roost.

Many types of mother bats turn themselves right-side up and hang from their thumb claws during birth. The mother catches her baby in her tail membrane, then turns upside down again and holds the newborn under her wing to nurse. Unlike many other types of bats, flying foxes often give birth while upside down and catch the young in their wings.

Infant flying foxes hang on to their mothers all the time—even when their mothers fly. After the first few weeks, though, the young are too heavy for that. Young flying foxes then hang by their claws from a branch when their mothers search for fruit.

Some other types of bats, especially those that hunt for food instead of feeding on fruit, never carry their young. They always leave their young to hang within a cave, crevice, or other hiding place.

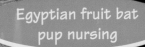

Egyptian fruit bat
pup nursing

Why Do Some Bats Like Caves?

Caves are the preferred housing for many kinds of animals. Bats use caves because they offer shelter, a fairly constant temperature, many different places to roost, and protection from predators.

Different species of bats like to use caves differently. Some fruit bats hang close to a cave's entrance, so that they can easily fly out and look for fruit. But other bats, such as vampire and horseshoe bats, fly farther back into the dark recesses of caves to find places to roost.

Some types of bats like to squeeze into cracked rocks or crevices, including the insides of hollowed-out logs. Many bats even roost in attics and other human-made structures.

Egyptian fruit bats
hanging in a cave

Who Has a Summer Home and a Winter Home?

A type of bat known as the little brown bat can be found throughout the United States and Canada. During the summer, these bats spend the day roosting in caves, attics, or other shelters. At night, they come out to hunt for insects.

When autumn comes, little brown bats fly to their winter roosts. The winter roost may be fairly close to the summer roost. Little brown bats do not usually fly south, as do most birds and some other kinds of bats. Instead, they fly to large caves and abandoned mines, where they spend the winter. A large abandoned mine may hold up to 300,000 roosting little brown bats. Little brown bats return to the same winter homes for many generations.

Bat flying out
of a cave

33

Who Flies South for the Winter?

Unlike the little brown bat discussed on the prior two pages, many other bats, including the Mexican free-tailed bat, follow migrating patterns much like those of birds. They travel hundreds of miles each spring and fall.

Most Mexican free-tailed bats spend their summers in the southern United States and in Mexico, where they roost in caves and human-made structures. They live in colonies that may include several hundred bats each. The largest colonies are made up of mothers and young.

As the days grow shorter and the weather cools, most of the adult Mexican free-tailed bats and their grown young fly to southern Mexico and Central America. Since the young are born in June, they are old enough to make the migration with their colony when it's time to leave in the fall. In spring, most of the Mexican free-tailed bats make the long trip north again.

34

Migration of Mexican
free-tailed bats

Who Likes to Camp Out?

Tent-building bats and white bats of the wet forests of Central and South America make themselves little A-frame tents in which to roost. There, they find shelter from violent rainstorms, sun, and predators.

To make their homes, these bats bite ridges into the underside of large leaves belonging to a plant called *Heliconia.* This plant has tough leaves that fold neatly along the ridges into a tent shape. Once they have made their tent, a group of bats gets under it and hangs on.

A single large leaf can provide shelter for over 20 bats. A colony of bats may make numerous leaf tents throughout a forest.

White bats
under a leaf

Who Lives in Houses?

Though many people are not fond of bats, some bats do not mind living close to people. Little and big brown bats, for example, like to live indoors. They often find shelter in caves, but sometimes they live in sheds, barns, garages, or even houses. Mexican free-tailed bats roost in houses, too.

Evening bats actually seem to prefer houses—although you also can find them in tree hollows. These bats are not the only bats to live in houses. Dozens of kinds of bats find good roosting places there. Some bats are small enough to squeeze into such tiny spaces as gaps between bricks and under eaves. Any place they can go to escape predators and the weather will work.

Little brown bats
roosting in a barn

Who Roosts Alone?

Bats enjoy many different kinds of roosting places. Some bats, such as the pallid bat of the American Southwest, will hide in just about any outdoor crevice. But they will form a small colony in an indoor space, as well.

Like pallid bats, most bats are social and roost in colonies. Some, however, are more solitary and prefer to hide alone in small, outdoor spaces. The silver-haired bat often hides alone in the bark of a tree or in an abandoned woodpecker's hole. Sometimes, silver-haired bats will roost in sheds or garages, but usually only when these buildings are open or abandoned.

Red bats and hoary bats also like to be alone. Both like to rest in the thick foliage of hardwood trees. You might mistake a red bat resting alone in a tree for a dead leaf.

Pallid bat

How Long Will Those Bats Hang There?

Bats that live in cooler climates hibernate through the winter. Their heartbeat slows. Their rate of breathing lowers so much that it can seem as if they have stopped breathing. Their bodies cool to match the temperature of their shelter. They spend the winter in a deep sleep. Hibernation helps bats survive until the weather is milder and food is more plentiful.

Sometimes a bat must wake from hibernation to move from a disturbed roost or to drink water. Waking can cause a bat to use up the energy it had stored as fat for the winter. A bat that is awakened several times might not survive the winter.

In spring, when the air temperature warms up, the bat will shiver and shake itself awake. It will stretch its legs and its wings and then venture out of the cave in search of food.

Lesser horseshoe
bat hibernating

Who's an Expert Bug Zapper?

The little brown bat—one of the most common bats in North America—can eat more than its own body weight in insects in only one night.

The little brown bat can eat hundreds of mosquitoes a night. Its relative, the big brown bat, can eat hundreds of beetles a night.

It has been estimated that a large colony of Mexican free-tailed bats can eat over 200 tons (some 200,000 kilograms) of insects in a single night.

Although many orchard owners consider fruit bats to be pests, nearly all farmers appreciate other bats for their ability to help control insects.

Little brown bat
eating a moth

Who Fishes for a Living?

Fisherman bats fly over the calm lakes, rivers, and even the seacoasts of Mexico and South America in search of food. They are good at locating it, too. They can catch over 30 fish in a single night!

A fisherman bat uses echolocation to sense the ripples that fish make when they approach the surface of the water. Then the bat dives down and hooks the fish using the large claws on its feet. Sometimes the bat eats its fish as it flies, but the bat may fly off to roost in a safe place to enjoy its meal.

Like ducks with oily feathers, fisherman bats have oily fur that sheds water. Without this oil, their fur might become too wet, and the weight of the water might make the bats too heavy to fly. But, with their special fur, if these bats get splashed, they simply shake the water away. If a fisherman bat somehow falls into the water, it can use its wings to swim to safety.

Fisherman bat feeding on a fish

Who Listens for the Sound of Dinner?

Unlike most meat-eating bats that use echolocation to find their prey, frog-eating bats simply listen for calling frogs. When they hear frogs croaking out mating songs, the bats home in on the sound.

Frog-eating bats can tell the difference between the calls of poisonous frogs and those of harmless ones. So, they hunt for the frogs that are edible.

In addition to eating frogs, a few species of bats eat lizards, rodents, small birds, and other bats. Some bats can even catch fish with their claws. Most bats eat insects.

Frog-eating bat
and its prey

Are Some Bats Vampires?

A few kinds of bats feed on the blood of other mammals. These bats are called vampire bats.

Common vampire bats, which live in Mexico and South America, feed on the blood of horses, cattle, and fowl (birds such as chickens). Although it is rare, vampire bats can also feed on human blood.

A vampire bat searches for a sleeping animal. Then it lands nearby and climbs onto the animal. The bat uses its teeth to cut away the fur of the animal and quickly makes a small cut into the victim's skin. Its teeth are so sharp that the sleeping animal doesn't even feel the cut.

Once an animal starts bleeding, the vampire bat uses its tongue to lap up blood from the wound.

Vampire bat

51

Does a Vampire Bat Kill Its Prey?

Vampire bats are very small mammals. They usually weigh about 1 ounce (28 grams). Their wingspan might measure 12 inches (30.5 centimeters) across. They eat only about 1 tablespoon (15 milliliters) of blood a day. Most animals never notice that they've been bitten by a vampire bat.

Sometimes, however, several vampire bats feed on the same animal at once. If the animal is small or sick, it can grow weak and even die from blood loss.

The greater danger, though, is that vampire bats often spread diseases to their victims. If a vampire bat drinks the blood of an animal that has a disease, the bat can then carry the germs of that disease and spread them to other animals it bites. Sometimes the bat itself can become sick, as well.

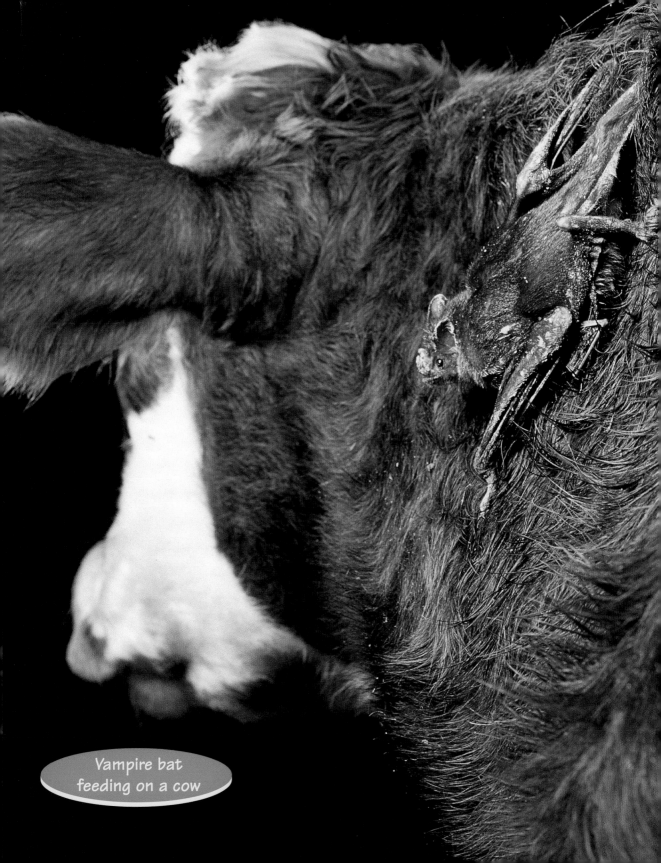

Vampire bat
feeding on a cow

Do Bats Carry Rabies?

Rabies is a disease that infects and kills all types of mammals. Many people think it is common for a bat to get rabies and survive it, becoming a carrier of the killer disease. But that is not quite true.

Bats rarely get rabies, but when they do, it kills them. However, a bat with rabies will usually die quietly rather than becoming obviously sick as some other mammals do. So, it is wise never to pick up a wild bat, even if it appears injured and in need of help. If frightened, the sick bat may bite and spread a disease to you.

Scientists and other animal handlers use heavy gloves when touching a bat, until they know for sure that the animal is free of disease.

Researcher holding a bat

Who Are a Bat's Predators?

Because they can fly, roost in hard-to-reach places, and are nocturnal, bats are safe from most predators. And most predators will not bother with a single bat, because it is too small to make much of a meal.

But snakes, raccoons, opossums, skunks, and even tarantulas prey on bats that they find roosting in trees or crevices. Hawks and owls can sometimes catch bats in midair. A young bat that falls from its roost may be eaten by the insects that live on the floor of the cave.

Another danger faced by bats comes from parasites. Parasites are organisms that live off of other animals' bodies. For example, tiny ticks, mites, and fleas can attach themselves to a bat's body and live off its blood. Often, parasites can make a bat weak and sick.

Tarantula feeding
on a bat

How Do Bats Help Humans?

Having insect-eating bats around can be better than having an electronic bug-zapper. In fact, humans often try to attract bats to their backyards by providing bat houses. A bat house is a small box that resembles a birdhouse, which gives bats a safe place to roost.

Bats are helpful in other ways, too. They spread seeds and pollinate plants. Even their waste, which is called guano, is useful. Bat droppings return nutrients to the soil of their habitats. Guano is even "mined" from the floor of large caves. It is then used by farmers as fertilizer.

Bat house
surrounded by bats

Are Bats in Danger?

Some kinds of bats are common, but others are rare or endangered. Some are already extinct. Though they do not have many natural predators, some bats are threatened by humans.

People who fear bats often destroy their habitats. Sometimes fruit growers kill fruit bats to keep them from eating their crops. Ranchers kill vampire bats to protect their livestock, too. And bats that roost in trees lose their habitats when forests are cut down.

In Asia, bats are sometimes killed for food. Even cave explorers who mean the bats no harm can accidentally disturb their roosts.

In several countries, efforts have been made to help bats survive. For example, in the United States several large caves and abandoned mines have been protected. Some of these places have been fitted with gates that keep humans out but let bats in. Several Asian flying foxes are considered endangered and are protected by international laws.

Little red flying foxes clustered on a branch

Bat Fun Facts

→ Some scientists think that flying foxes and other fruit bats are more closely related to primates (such mammals as humans and apes) than they are to other bats.

→ Bats groom themselves as cats do. Bats frequently wash their faces and then fluff up their fur.

→ A newborn bat may weigh nearly half as much as its mother.

→ Rousette fruit bats echolocate differently than do most bats. Instead of making high-pitched squeaks and clicks in their voice boxes, they click and clack with their tongues.

→ According to the fossil record, bats have looked almost the same for the past 50 million years.

→ Scientists have proved that bats have been roosting in Carlsbad Caverns in New Mexico for 17,000 years.

Glossary

colony A large group of animals living together.

echolocation The use of high-pitched sounds to find food and avoid hitting things in the dark.

endangered In danger of extinction, or dying out.

guano The bodily waste of bats, which can be used as fertilizer.

habitat The area where an animal lives, such as a forest.

hardwood A tree with tough, hard wood that loses its leaves every autumn, such as an oak tree.

hibernate To sleep through the cold months.

insectivorous To eat mainly insects.

mammal A member of a group of animals that give birth to live young; the newborns drink their mothers' milk.

migrate To travel from one region to another with a change in the season.

nectar The sugary liquid inside flowers that some bats eat.

nocturnal To be active during the night.

nursery roost The place where a mother bat gives birth.

parasite An organism that lives off of another organism, often causing illness.

pollen A powdery substance that unites with egg cells inside a flower, leading to the production of seeds.

pollinate To carry pollen from one flower to another, enabling the second flower to produce seeds.

predator An animal that hunts and eats other animals.

rabies A deadly disease spread by some animals that destroys part of the brain.

roost For a bat to sleep—or the place where a bat sleeps.

tail membrane The skin on the sides of a bat's tail.

Index

(**Boldface** indicates a photo, map, or illustration.)

For more information about Flying Foxes and Other Bats, try these resources:

Amazing Bats, by Frank Greenaway, Alfred A. Knopf, 1991.

Bats, by Sue Ruff and Don E. Wilson, Benchmark Books, 2000.

Flying Foxes: Fruit and Blossom Bats of Australia, by Leslie Hall and Greg Richards, Krieger, 2001.

http://www.batconservation.org/
http://www.bats.org.uk/
http://www.bellingen.com/flyingfoxes/

Bat Classification

Scientists classify animals by placing them into groups. The animal kingdom is a group that contains all the world's animals. Phylum, class, order, and family are smaller groups. Each phylum contains many classes. A class contains orders, an order contains families, and a family contains individual species. Each species also has its own scientific name. (The abbreviation "spp." after a genus name indicates that a group of species from a genus is being discussed.) Here is how the animals in this book fit in to this system.

Animals with backbones and their relatives (Phylum Chordata)

Mammals (Class Mammalia)

Bats (Order Chiroptera)

Large bats (Suborder Megachiroptera)

Flying foxes and other fruit bats (Family Pteropodidae)

Aldabra flying fox	*Pteropus aldabrensis*
Indian flying fox	*Pteropus giganteus*
Little red flying fox	*Pteropus scapulatus*
Spectacled flying fox	*Pteropus conspicillatus*
Rousette fruit bats	*Rousettus* spp.
Egyptian fruit bat	*Rousettus aegyptiacus*

Small bats (Suborder Microchiroptera)

Fisherman bats (Family Noctilionidae)

Free-tailed bats (Family Molossidae)

Mexican free-tailed bat	*Tadarida brasiliensis*

Horseshoe bats (Family Rhinolophidae)

Lesser horseshoe bat	*Rhinolophus hipposideros*

Leaf-nosed bats (Family Phyllostomidae)

Common vampire bat	*Desmodus rotundus*
Frog-eating bat	*Trachops cirrhosus*
Tent-building bats	*Uroderma* spp.
White bat	*Ectophylla alba*

Kitti's hog-nosed bat (Family Craseonycteridae)

Kitti's hog-nosed bat	*Craseonycteris thonglongyai*

Vespertilionid bats (Family Vespertilionidae)

Big brown bat	*Eptesicus fuscus*
Evening bat	*Nycticeius humeralis*
Hoary bat	*Lasiurus cinereus*
Red bat	*Lasiurus borealis*
Little brown bats	*Myotis* spp.
Long-eared bats	*Plecotus* spp.
Pallid bat	*Antrozous pallidus*
Silver-haired bat	*Lasionycteris noctivagans*